YOUR PERSONALITY AND YOU
JOURNAL

YOUR PERSONALITY AND YOU

JOURNAL

Prompts and Practices to Better Understand Yourself, Reflect, and Grow

AGNES WARD, PhD

ROCKRIDGE PRESS

For general information on our other products and services, please contact our Customer Care Department within the United States at (866) 744-2665, or outside the United States at (510) 253-0500.

Paperback ISBN: 978-1-63878-458-6

Manufactured in the United States of America

Interior and Cover Designer: John Calmeyer
Art Producer: Melissa Malinowsky
Editor: Brian Sweeting
Production Editor: Jax Berman
Production Manager: Holly Haydash

Illustrations © LEROY Design/Creative Market

10 9 8 7 6 5 4 3 2 1

This book belongs to

CONTENTS

INTRODUCTION viii

HOW TO USE THIS JOURNAL ix

PART I Taking an Honest Look at Yourself and Your Past 1

PART II Setting Goals with a Purpose 27

PART III Taking Action and Forming the Habits You Want 55

PART IV Keeping Track of Your Growth 83

PART V Tackling Obstacles and Failing Well 111

PART VI Practicing Self-Love 139

RESOURCES 166

REFERENCES 168

INDEX 170

INTRODUCTION

Welcome! I'm so glad you're here. I'm Agnes Ward, a licensed psychologist, certified advanced alcohol and drug counselor, and licensed behavior analyst. I've helped many people become the person they want to be. As you work through this journal, you'll be amazed by what you learn about yourself and the progress you'll make toward your goals.

I'll guide you through the steps that will help you better understand yourself, reflect, and grow. Whether you're working on setting and achieving goals, changing certain habits, overcoming obstacles, or learning to love yourself, this journal will serve as your guide.

My journey to becoming a psychologist began as I sat on my bed with two acceptance letters to graduate programs: one for communication and the other for psychology. I went with my true passion and enrolled in the psychology program. My professional journey has led me to helping people with trauma and addiction. Later, I discovered I could help people even more by teaching them how to change their *behaviors* and achieve the life they want.

If you feel stuck and are having difficulty making changes in your life, keep reading. Growth and change might feel scary or daunting, but with effort and determination, change *is* possible. You can do it! I'll show you how.

HOW TO USE THIS JOURNAL

This journal is divided into six parts. The first gives you the opportunity to take an honest look at yourself and your life so far. Next, you'll look at setting goals with a purpose. After that, you'll be invited to take action to form the habits you want. Then, you'll learn how to keep track of progress and tackle obstacles along the way. The last part asks you to work on increasing your self-love.

Although this journal is designed to be completed in order, feel free to jump around if a particular part is more meaningful or useful to you right now. After all, this is your journal, and there's no wrong way to use it. Just make sure you work through all six parts to get the full benefit and to gain a deeper understanding of yourself. You may even choose to revisit certain parts multiple times.

This journal is a companion to *Your Personality and You Workbook* (Rockridge Press, 2022). You may want to purchase this workbook as a companion guide and additional resource, but this book functions perfectly well on its own.

Let's Talk About Personality

When people talk about making changes, they're often referring to their personality. But what exactly *is* personality? Some define it as the way someone behaves. Such adjectives as "responsible," "sensitive," "reckless," or "arrogant" might be used to describe personality. In psychology, "personality" refers to the traits that drive individuals to think, feel, and behave in consistent ways (McCrae and Costa 2003).

Though personality is defined by traits that reflect consistent styles of thinking, feeling, and behaving, we are not necessarily stuck with our personalities. We've all heard stories about people overcoming all kinds of challenges and obstacles in their lives: people overcoming addiction, making changes to reach a desired weight, or achieving a healthier lifestyle. You might have heard about people reaching out to estranged family members and reconnecting. Accounts of people overcoming anxiety, depression, and other negative mood states also exist. You may have seen such stories in the media, or perhaps someone you know has experienced such improvement. Personalities can and do change!

How does change occur? Think of personality change as a process. It happens over time, not overnight. You didn't become the person you are in a week, and your thoughts, feelings, and behaviors didn't develop in a day. Rather, they likely took years, if not your entire life, to develop. However, self-awareness, setting goals, and taking specific actions can bring change for you, starting now.

PERSONALITY TESTS AND WHAT THEY MEAN

You might have heard of personality tests or even taken one. They measure the traits that people exhibit across a variety of situations and are used in academic, clinical, and educational settings.

Many different personality tests or inventories have been created. One of the most widely used is the Big Five Inventory–2 (BFI–2). It assesses the "Big Five" personality traits: agreeableness, conscientiousness, extraversion, negative emotionality, and open-mindedness. Another inventory, the Minnesota Multiphasic Personality Inventory (MMPI), assesses symptoms of mental illness and maladaptive personality traits. The latest version, MMPI-2-RF, includes scales related to aggression, self-doubt, social avoidance, and other specific problems. The Hogan Personality Inventory (HPI), based on the Big Five, is used to predict work performance. HPI's scales are organized by work-relevant characteristics, such as ambition, interpersonal sensitivity, and sociability. The Myers-Briggs Type Indicator (MBTI) uses the assignment of a "type," summarized in four of eight possible letters: extraversion (E) or introversion (I), sensing (S) or intuiting (N), thinking (T) or feeling (F), and judging (J) or perceiving (P). It is widely used in the business setting.

Although these personality inventories are among the most valid and reliable, be mindful when using them or any other personality tests; they identify traits, not a person's potential, drives, motivations, or ability to change. For that reason, they should be used as tools to help you understand yourself in this moment and not to solidify your fate.

PART I

Taking an Honest Look at Yourself and Your Past

*Making a big life change is scary,
but you know what's even scarier? Regret.*

—ZIG ZIGLAR

In this part of the journal, you'll take an honest look at yourself and your past. To make positive changes, you first need to understand yourself and what has made you the person you are today. Have you always been the way you are now? Or did an event in your life change you? Maybe it was a person or a series of experiences. Reflecting on these points will help you to get to know yourself better so you can move forward. It might be difficult, and even scary, to really think about the person you are. Maybe you've avoided this type of introspective thinking for a long time, but to accomplish positive change, you have to be honest with yourself no matter how uncomfortable it might be. The prompts and practices in this part of the journal will help you evaluate your thoughts, feelings, and behaviors as well as the ways they have shaped the person you are today. Acknowledging the experiences in your life and how they have affected you will allow you to move forward.

Who are you? What characteristics do you apply to yourself? Write down the first few words that come to mind, and be honest. Everyone has qualities they feel are positive as well as those they hope to change. Next to each characteristic, note whether it is positive, negative, or neutral. Describe how the traits you listed about yourself have contributed to certain situations and circumstances in your life right now.

____

____

____

____

____

____

____

____

____

____

____

____

SELF-AWARENESS ABOUT CHANGE

This exercise will help you reflect on the person you are and on your thoughts about changing. Because change can be scary, it's helpful to evaluate what exactly changing means to you and whether making changes in your life would be better than keeping things as they are. Be honest with yourself as you fill in the blanks that follow. This is the start of your journey and of you preparing to choose your path forward.

1. When I think about who I am, I feel _______________________________.

2. The most concerning thing about my personality is _______________________________.

3. If I continue to do the things I do, the result will be _______________________________.

4. When I think about changing, I feel _______________________________.

5. The scariest thing about change is _______________________________.

6. If I don't make any changes in my life, the end result will be _______________________________.

7. Making changes in my life will result in _______________________________.

8. The things that prevent me from making changes are _______________________________.

9. If I'm going to change, I need to _______________________________.

10. A support person I can talk to is _______________________________.

*The mind is a flexible mirror, adjust it,
to see a better world.*

—AMIT RAY

Think about the person you are. This might sound like a big ask, but consider your good and bad qualities. A number of factors shape who we are, and many of us attribute some traits we possess to our parents(s). List two or three traits you believe you have inherited from your parent(s). Would you describe these traits as favorable, unfavorable, or neutral?

CONTINUED ▶

As a child or teenager, you may have had dreams of choosing a certain career, living in a particular place, or becoming a spouse or parent. Describe which of those dreams (or parts of those dreams) you've fulfilled and which are left to conquer. Consider what might be preventing you from fulfilling those dreams, and include that, too. How might your feelings about yourself be different if you had fulfilled those dreams?

CONTINUED ▶

We may not always see ourselves the way others do. For example, you might think of yourself as a sensitive person who feels deeply, but you hide this side of yourself from others because you don't want to seem vulnerable.

In the first column in the chart that follows, list words that describe the way you see yourself. In the second column, list some words that describe how you think others see you. In the last column, fill in how you wish it to be. Be honest about this reflection.

HOW YOU SEE YOURSELF	HOW OTHERS SEE YOU	HOW YOU WISH IT TO BE

Is there a contrast between how you see yourself and how others see you? If so, how do you feel about that contrast?

____

What evidence do you have that others see you the way you've indicated?

____

How would your life be different if your wish came true so that you and others saw you as described in the third column?

____

FEELING ASSESSMENT

Actions have an impact not only on the people around us but also on the way we feel about ourselves. Think about a feeling or behavior you want to change in your life. Assess how engaging in your behaviors makes you feel. In turn, think about behaviors you might want to change that are associated with certain feelings or emotions. An example might be drinking alcohol and then feeling depressed because you drank too much. The following list will help you evaluate the feelings that follow the behaviors you want to change. Check the ones that apply to you.

When you engage in the behavior you want to change, how do you feel?

☐ Like I've failed

☐ That I'm not good enough

☐ Hopeless

☐ That I will never change

☐ Worthless

☐ Alone

☐ That I've disappointed people around me

☐ Like I'm not wanted

☐ Like people don't want to be around me

☐ Like I can't control myself

☐ Like people around me don't understand me

☐ That I have to act in a certain way or be perfect

☐ That there's something wrong with me

☐ Other:

____

The way we think affects the way we feel, and feelings influence the way we behave. Write down how you feel most of the time (for example, happy, sad, or angry). Is this the way you want to feel? Do you view yourself as an optimist, a pessimist, or somewhere in between? Describe how your thoughts and feelings contribute not only to the decisions you make but to the way you feel about these decisions afterward.

____

____

____

____

____

____

____

____

____

____

____

____

____

CONTINUED ▶

Every behavior serves a purpose. We take certain actions, regardless if we like these actions, in order to get something we want. Think about the behaviors you engage in that you're not happy with. List behaviors and describe what you get out of them (for example, you tend to be short with a co-worker to make them go away).

CONTINUED

CONTINUED ▶

Our actions have a profound impact on the people we love. Perhaps you haven't spoken to someone you care about for years, and you wish this weren't so. Write down the names of people you care about whom you've hurt. How do they respond to you when you act in ways that hurt them? Describe how you feel about their response. Do you worry about losing these relationships?

CONTINUED ▶

Sometimes we get stuck in a pattern of blaming others for who we are. This blame can prevent our own growth and change. Think about a person you blame for shaping who you are. Write down what you'd like to change about yourself as a result. How has this blame contributed to your feeling stuck in your life? Describe what it would mean to forgive. What would it take to get there?

____

____

____

____

____

____

____

____

____

____

____

CONTINUED ▶

Thinking about the past might bring up uncomfortable or distressing feelings. You might feel like the emotions are hard to control and that they get in the way of your relationships. In order to ground yourself or connect yourself back to the present when you're experiencing difficult feelings, try any of these exercises if you are able:

- Touch a blanket or other soft item, focusing on its texture.

- Wash your face with cold water or allow cold water to run on your hands and wrists.

- Eat or drink something healthy and experience the taste.

- Take a stroll and focus closely on the sounds you hear.

- Inhale slowly through your nose, relaxing your shoulders. Exhale slowly through your mouth. Repeat this a few times until you start to feel better.

- Look at where you are right now and take note of what you see, hear, smell, taste, and feel if you are able.

- Count backward from one hundred by fives. Concentrating on the counting will help you refocus, giving feelings a time-out.

To move forward it may be helpful to discuss your past with someone you trust and to consider the ways what's happened in the past has contributed to who you are today. Have you ever talked with someone else about your past? Maybe you're not sure how, and it feels scary to take that step. Remember that working on yourself isn't always easy, but doing so is worth the effort.

First choose a supportive and understanding person you trust to talk to. This person can be a family member or friend. Find a time when you're both free from distractions and use one or more of the following prompts to structure your conversation:

- *I've been reflecting a lot on my past recently.*

- *There are some things I wanted to ask/tell you about my past.*

- *I feel that much of what I do relates to experiences from my past.*

- *Some things about the past have been bothering me.*

- *I've been trying to let go of the past, and I'm wondering if you can help me.*

Think about a person who inspires you. It could be someone you know or a celebrity. Describe what you admire about this person and how they inspire you. Think about the traits they have that you wish you had. Do you think you have any traits in common with this person? If so, what are they? Describe the changes you can make to become more like this person.

CONTINUED ▶

Change can be hard. Just as getting better at a sport or instrument takes time and practice, the same is true of most tasks. Perhaps you've tried to make changes in your life, but you keep reverting to old habits. Make a two-column list: On one side, list the consequences of continuing to behave in the same way. On the other side, list the benefits of the changes you want to make.

CONTINUED ▶

Having an end goal in mind can be a motivating factor to keep you working on making the changes you want. If you successfully made such changes, what would be different in your life? How would you know that you succeeded in making the change? Describe how your relationships would change, considering whether people would perceive you differently. Would this improve your life and relationships?

PART II

Setting Goals with a Purpose

This one step—choosing a goal and sticking to it—changes everything.

—SCOTT REED

Now that you've taken a look at yourself and identified some of what makes you the person you are, we turn in this part of the journal to learning how to set goals so you can learn to be more like the person you want to be. Goals serve as your road map to defining and measuring progress. Writing down what you want to change about yourself helps solidify your intentions and reinforces your commitment to making changes. For example, if you want to quit smoking, you might set a goal to either pick a date to quit altogether or to decrease the number of cigarettes you smoke each day, and then stick to that number. Goals provide you with the opportunity to measure progress and take accountability for your actions. Breaking down goals into smaller, more specific parts often allows you to more easily measure your progress and stay on track. Incremental accomplishments can also give you a sense of victory over the habits you've been trying to change.

A great way to gain perspective is to write a story about how your life could have been. Describe a specific point in your life when you could have gone in a different direction. Consider what led you to where you are today. You can't change the past, of course, but writing about what you can do in the present, while considering your past actions, will help you avoid returning to a place you don't want to be.

PLANNING FOR CHANGE

It's helpful to define exactly what you want to change and why and to imagine the effect that might come from this change. For example, maybe you want to decrease your anxiety because it hinders your relationships with others, but you're afraid to take the steps to make the change. Contemplating the following questions will help you examine your behavior in more depth as well as the potential consequences of not changing in order to consider the help you might need.

1. Define the problem in as much detail as possible.

2. How would another person you know define this problem?

3. How are you responsible for your problem? When did it start?

4. What are the possible ways to address this problem?

5. Will the problem you're trying to address go away on its own?

6. What steps can you take to change it?

7. What is the worst possible outcome if you do nothing about it?

8. If you choose to do nothing, will it matter a month from now?

9. Is anyone you know worried about this problem?

10. Can anyone help you with this problem?

11. What fears do you have if you don't resolve the problem?

A 2019 textbook by authors John Cooper, Timothy E. Heron, and William Heward posits that the ways people behave serve four main functions: to get attention, to escape or avoid a situation, to experience a pleasant sensation, and to gain access to something wanted.

Take an honest look at yourself and the behaviors you engage in. For example, you might bite your nails because it helps release tension. Complete the table that follows by filling in the behaviors for each function category.

BEHAVIORS TO GET ATTENTION	BEHAVIORS TO ESCAPE OR AVOID
1.	1.
2.	2.
3.	3.

BEHAVIORS TO EXPERIENCE A PLEASANT SENSATION	BEHAVIORS TO GAIN ACCESS TO SOMETHING WANTED
1.	1.
2.	2.
3.	3.

Now, list at least three replacement behaviors for each category. These are positive behaviors to substitute for more favorable outcomes.

REPLACEMENT BEHAVIORS TO GET ATTENTION	REPLACEMENT BEHAVIORS TO ESCAPE OR AVOID
1.	1.
2.	2.
3.	3.

REPLACEMENT BEHAVIORS THAT BRING PLEASANT SENSATIONS	REPLACEMENT BEHAVIORS THAT PROVIDE ACCESS
1.	1.
2.	2.
3.	3.

A vision of the future can help motivate you to make necessary changes now. Picturing what your life will be like when you succeed in making the changes you want can help you set a plan to get there. Describe what you want your life to look like in five years. How do you want people to see you? When they describe you, what do you want them to say?

____

____

____

____

____

____

____

____

____

____

____

____

CONTINUED ▶

Many people attempt to make changes more than once. Have you? If so, write down what successes you've had. Describe what worked for you and how long the change lasted. Consider who in your life helped support you. Now, describe what didn't work and what got you off the path of change. Consider whether those factors are still around in your life and if they might be sabotaging your progress.

CONTINUED ▶

Setting and implementing goals often requires a change in lifestyle. Make a list of some of what will need to change in order for you to make progress. What emotions come to mind when you think about giving up certain things you might associate with comfort? Describe any feelings of loss that could make this change difficult. Compare the pros and cons of changing your lifestyle.

CONTINUED ▶

To increase your chances of success, set goals that are specific, measurable, achievable, relevant, and timely. Write down your goal in the space provided, and go through the checklist to make sure it's S.M.A.R.T (a tool created by George T. Doran in 1981 in an issue of *Management Review*). Adjust your goal until you've included each element. Repeat the process for additional goals if you wish.

GOAL:____

☐ **Is this goal Specific?**	Define the goal in detail. What do you want to accomplish and why? Who will be involved? Where will you work on it? What constraints might you have?
☐ **Is this goal Measurable?**	How will you measure your progress, and how will you know you've accomplished your goal?
☐ **Is this goal Achievable?**	What logical action steps will you take to achieve this goal?
☐ **Is this goal Relevant?**	Does this goal align with your long-term objectives? Is this the right time to change, and do you have the resources to accomplish this goal?
☐ **Is this goal Timely?**	What is the target date of achieving this goal? Is there a daily or weekly amount of time you will devote to working on this goal?

When setting goals, think of a specific person or people in your life who can cheer you on (this could be a partner, spouse, co-worker, or friend). Why do they come to mind? How can you ask them to help you become more accountable for your actions and check in with you about your progress? Talking about your plan out loud can solidify it and motivate you to work harder.

All kinds of obstacles can get in the way of achieving goals, such as work schedules, daily tasks, ongoing obligations, and unexpected events. When making changes, it's helpful to prepare for possible setbacks and have a detailed plan to overcome them. It can be challenging to stop engaging in certain behaviors, so having a plan for dealing with setbacks can help keep you from reverting to old habits. A great idea is to enlist the help of family members or friends to help you monitor your progress and provide support if they think you might be slipping. Complete the following table, reflecting on possible setbacks. Develop a plan of action around what you'll do if you start wandering off your path to change.

WHAT MIGHT INTERFERE WITH MY PROGRESS	WHAT I CAN DO TO STAY ON TRACK	SUPPORT I NEED DURING THIS TIME

*Setting goals is the first step in turning
the invisible into the visible.*

—TONY ROBBINS

Examining your motivation and mindset can have a huge impact on your efforts to achieve your goals. On a scale from 1 to 10 (10 = most motivated), rate your motivation level for achieving your goal. Think about your ability to take the steps needed to change and be honest with yourself. Are you all in? Are the goals truly yours? These factors will be important indicators of the progress you'll make.

CONTINUED ▶

No one's perfect. Most people try to change their habits multiple times before they succeed. Describe in detail what you need to do to stay on track (for example, being patient with yourself, measuring your progress, and making adjustments as you go). Make a list of the steps you'll take if you feel like giving up at some point. Doing this in advance will help you stay focused and keep your goals in sight.

CONTINUED ▶

Maybe you know what changes you'd like to make but you don't know where to start. For example, let's say you want to change your diet but you're not sure which one to try. Assess your knowledge about what you need to do to change. Write down what you think will work. Consider whether you need the support of family, friends, or professionals. List the resources you imagine you might need.

CONTINUED ▶

Setting goals to change can be intimidating and may even feel scary. But your chances of success increase when your plan involves making changes enjoyable (and even fun), recognizing your successes, and making adjustments as needed. Get creative! Describe a plan that makes a change more appealing to you. For example, instead of setting a goal to stop eating sweets, plan to replace them with a healthy, delicious smoothie.

CONTINUED ▶

LIFE AFTER GOAL ACHIEVEMENT

Envisioning what your life might be like after you make the desired changes can help motivate you to stay focused (de Shazer et al. 2021). Doing so often can keep you motivated. It's helpful to have a clear vision of your life changing for the better. This exercise will help you visualize in detail how achieving your goal will improve your life.

If you solved your problem:

1. How will you know your problem is solved? _______________________________________

2. How will your friends and family know your problem is solved without you telling them? _______________________________________

3. How will solving your problem change your relationships? _______________________

4. How will solving your problem change your situation at work? _______________

5. How will solving your problem affect your health? _______________________________

6. How will solving your problem affect your mood? _______________________________

7. Will solving your problem have an impact on your self-esteem? _______________

8. Will solving your problem change the way you view your life? _______________

As you set your goals for change, consider whether they are tied to someone else's. It's important to acknowledge that we can't control anyone but ourselves. Have you tied your progress to someone else's goals or to their vision of what your life should be like? If so, think about why. List the possible consequences of making changes for someone else rather than yourself.

____

____

____

____

____

____

____

____

____

____

____

____

PART III

Taking Action and Forming the Habits You Want

*You don't have to be great to get started,
but you have to get started to be great.*

—LES BROWN

Now that you've learned more about yourself and how to set goals to put you on the path to success, we'll turn in this part of the journal to how to take action. Think about what you do: Your typical behavior pattern probably doesn't vary too much from day to day. If you don't take action to make changes, your goals become more like wishes or dreams. To get to where you want to be, you'll need a road map, or a well-defined action plan, directing you to your destination. This part of the book explores ways you can get started by motivating yourself, developing your plan, and successfully executing the changes you want to make.

Motivation is key to staying on track toward your goals. Describe your plan to stay motivated. Consider repeating a mantra every morning, such as "I can do this." You might also tell family and friends what goals you're working on. Write down any daily tasks that push you to take steps toward your goals, and make sure they're positive and even fun. The more enjoyable they are, the more achievable they'll be.

Positive affirmations can help you challenge negative thinking and keep you on track. Athletes often use positive self-talk to reduce anxiety and increase performance. The affirmations that follow can increase your positivity, self-confidence, and self-esteem, and they can help you achieve your goals.

Circle the affirmations that work best for you. You can even place one (or more) on your bathroom mirror where you'll see it as you begin your day. Repeating the affirmation is key to getting into the right mindset, and saying it out loud is the first step to believing it.

- I've got this.

- I'll get through this.

- I can learn to do this.

- I'm in control.

- I'm not giving up.

- I can work for this.

- I can let this go.

- I'm not giving up.

- I can try this a different way.

- I can forgive myself.

- I have the power to change.

- I can forgive those who hurt me.

- I deserve happiness.

- I am on the right track.

- I can try new things.

- I can do anything I set my mind to.

- I can choose to be happy.

- This is possible.

- I am confident.

Rate your level of happiness on a scale from 1 to 10 (10 = happiest). Make a list of the positive things in your life that make you happy. Specify how often you experience or engage in each of these. If your score is lower than you want it to be, write out some steps you can take to increase your engagement in activities that make you happy.

CONTINUED ▶

Every behavior has an antecedent and a consequence. The antecedent is what happens right before the behavior occurs, and the consequence is the result of behavior. Think about the habits you want to change and how antecedents and consequences are evident in your behaviors. Fill in the boxes that follow.

BEHAVIOR (behavior you would like to change)	ANTECEDENT (what happened right before the behavior occurred)	CONSEQUENCE (what happened immediately after the behavior occurred)

Have a look at the antecedents you listed. Are any of these within your control? If so, what can you do to avoid the antecedents to your behavior?

Now think about the consequences of your behaviors. How do your behaviors make you feel? Do they have a negative impact on you or your loved ones?

When the antecedents to your behavior are present, how can you act differently to change the consequences? Can you think of replacement behaviors for your current behaviors? Replacements should be positive.

Imagine starting to take action to achieve your goals. Who will notice first? Describe any thoughts you have about others noticing. Consider if having others paying attention motivates you to continue toward your goal, if it delays you from your efforts to work on yourself, or if it affects you in some other way. Maybe you fear that others will criticize, scrutinize, try to correct, or become overly involved in your action plan. Write down what this might look like and describe how you might counteract these unwelcome intrusions.

____

____

____

____

____

____

____

____

____

____

____

Think about your past relationships. Are any of them hindering your change process? Maybe you haven't had closure with someone who was in your life. Write down what you want that person to know. You might try writing a letter that you won't mail. Be honest and write down the feelings that come up. For example, you might feel hurt or sad because you didn't get what you'd wished for from the relationship.

Setting an action plan sometimes means losing relationships. What impact do you think your actions will have on your relationships? Write down any fears you have about losing relationships, even unhealthy ones, as you change. Consider how the person or people in these relationships contribute to your current stagnation. Would you say they care about you? Describe how. Think about whether they would support your plan to change, and what your prediction says about the relationship.

As you've worked through the prompts and exercises related to formulating a plan so far, you may have discovered a few strategies you'd like to try. An action plan is most effective when you gather all your available resources. Consider the people and tools that your action plan requires (for example, buying supplies, obtaining contact information, or getting rid of items). Make a resource list and create a plan, noting target dates, to obtain those resources.

Thinking about your strengths and areas where you may need improvement will help you as you prepare to make the changes you want. Are you determined, creative, great at organizing, or dependable? Consider how you can set goals around your identified strengths. This will help keep you motivated. Now think about your areas of growth that might hinder your progress, including personality traits that might be keeping you from reaching your goal. Let's say you want to be more social, but fear is keeping you from taking steps to meet new people. The following questions will help you identify your strengths and areas of growth, allowing you to plan around them.

Name five of your strengths that will help you accomplish your goal.

____

Name five strengths your friends or family would say you have.

____

Name five areas you need to work on because they're hindering your progress.

____

List three to five steps you need to take toward your goal.

____

____

Whom can you ask to get involved to help you with your identified goals?

____

Take Action! An inch of movement will bring you closer to your goals than a mile of intentions.

—DR. STEVE MARABOLI

Contemplating all you need to change can feel overwhelming. Think baby steps. Write down one or two things you can do right now to move toward change. For example, if you're trying to break a habit, what small step can you take? Maybe getting rid of something, making a purchase, or calling someone will get you closer to your goal.

____

____

____

____

____

____

____

____

____

____

CONTINUED ▶

One way to change old habits is to make them less convenient. So, if you want to stop drinking alcohol, get rid of what you have and don't keep any in the house. Describe some ways you can make old habits less desirable. Then, write down how you can make new habits more appealing.

CONTINUED ▶

It can take quite some time for change to take hold as new behaviors become second nature. It can be helpful, then, to work on new behaviors by breaking them down into small action steps. For example, to learn guitar, the action steps could be (1) take lessons, (2) set a practice schedule at home, and (3) practice. Focus on one or two small changes and commit to them for at least sixty days. If all goes well, work on another action step toward behavior change. This exercise will help you get started.

The first behavior I want to change is _______________________________________.

The first few action steps I need to take are

1. ____

2. ____

3. ____

My start date to work on the first action step is _______________________________.

I'll know I've made progress on this action step when ___________________________.

My start date to take the second action step is _________________________________.

I'll know I've made progress on this action step when ___________________________.

My start date to take the third action step is __________________________________.

I'll know I've made progress on this action step when ___________________________.

I'll continue to remind myself to monitor my progress on my first action step by _______

____

____.

BEHAVIOR CHANGE CONTRACT

A behavior change contract is an agreement you make with yourself that outlines what you expect yourself to do to change a behavior. Use this template to formalize your commitment to a behavior change.

- Name: ____

- The change I want to make is _______________________________.

- I want to change this behavior because _____________________.

- The action steps I need to take to change this behavior are

1. ____.

2. ____.

3. ____.

- The start date for making this change is ___________________.

- I'll know that I'm making progress when ___________________.

- I'll review my progress on a _______________________ (time frame) basis.

- If I make this behavior change within this time frame and by ___________ (end date),

  I'll reward myself by _____________________________________.

- If I don't follow this contract, then ______________________.

- Your Signature: ____.

- Witness Signature: ______________________________________.

Emotions can be difficult to change. Initially, you might consider a "fake it 'til you make it" approach by which you replace the emotion you want to change with its opposite. For example, if you're feeling sad, try smiling. Research shows that our facial muscles support our emotional experience (Coles et al. 2019). Write down the emotions and the substitutions to try. Make a list of the situations where you can use these.

CONTINUED ▶

Think about the changes you're making and note that self-esteem typically increases with positive movement. You may be focused largely on changes that impact people in your inner circle, but how would it feel to expand outward to include others, or even the planet? Consider, for example, volunteering, mentoring, recycling, or picking paper over plastic. Write down a few actions you can take to have a positive impact on the community and the environment.

CONTINUED ▶

PART IV

Keeping Track of Your Growth

*You cannot change your decision overnight,
but you can change your direction overnight.*

—JIM ROHN

You've taken action toward making the changes you want. To stay motivated, it's important to measure your progress in some way. Think of a time when you tried to make changes in your life but became discouraged because your approach didn't seem to be working. Perhaps you were making progress, but you didn't have a way to measure it. It's like training for a marathon but not keeping track of your improvements in time or distance.

This part of the journal suggests ways you can measure your progress and helps you determine what you need to do to reach your end goal. Keeping track of your growth will help you stay on track. As you work through these exercises, you may notice that changes you viewed as insignificant are actually important steps toward your goal. In this section, you'll also explore how to get through feelings of stagnation when you might be lacking motivation. You've come this far! Staying focused on your decision to make a change is well worth the effort.

Think about where you are today with the changes you've made so far. Reflect, too, on the beginning of your journey and describe how making changes makes you feel now. Consider your self-esteem, motivation, and belief in your own abilities. Summarize the progress you've made, and write down where you still need to go. What is your motivation level to continue?

Measuring your growth by regularly reflecting on where you were when you started your journey compared with where you are now can be very helpful. Use the exercise here to reflect on your progress and accomplishments so far.

What efforts have you made so far in your journey? Describe the behaviors you've changed and the ways you're measuring your progress.

____

____

What has changed in your life as a result of your progress? Describe any relationship changes you've experienced with loved ones, friends, or co-workers.

____

____

What have you learned about yourself so far? Write down the strengths you feel you have as well as the skills you've developed as a result of your growth (for example, the ability to say no or to avoid difficult people or situations).

____

____

What else needs to happen for you to accomplish your goal fully? For example, can you identify certain behaviors you feel you should stick with or perhaps stop? Do you have relationships that still need to change in some way?

____

____

Have you had a specific setback in your efforts to make the changes you want? Remember that setbacks are common and changing habits takes time. Maybe you stopped practicing a sport, or you're not communicating with a family member despite setting this as a goal. Think about and write down what gets you off track. Then list some actions you can take to continue your change journey when old patterns emerge.

CONTINUED ▶

As you notice success in making changes, you might feel your self-portrait or the way you see yourself changing. This exercise asks you to compare your earlier self, before you began making changes, to your current self.

First, in the left-hand frame, draw your past self. This can be a drawing of you or symbols that reflect who you were. Try to use descriptive images or symbols. For example, if you had low self-esteem, you might draw yourself as small.

Now, in the right-hand frame, draw the way you see yourself now. Maybe you feel more at peace and with improved self-esteem. You might draw yourself standing on top of a hill, symbolizing that you've conquered something.

PAST SELF-PORTRAIT	CURRENT SELF-PORTRAIT

Reflect on your drawings. Using feeling words, describe what comes to mind as you consider the differences between the two. For example, you might feel surprised, pleased, or proud.

Your self-talk or inner voice can help you continue moving forward, and it can also delay your progress. Describe your inner voice. Is it supportive, critical, or neutral? Then jot down the ways your inner voice has affected your change journey. Perhaps it has cheered you on, or maybe it's tried to convince you to give up. Give this some thought, and write down how you can use positive self-talk to encourage progress.

Part of the change process involves growth and wisdom from experiences and lessons learned. Growth comes when we take responsibility for our actions. Perhaps you blamed someone else for your problem but are now taking some responsibility for it. Taking responsibility can set us free by helping us release anger, resentment, hurt feelings, and other negative emotions. It can also improve and even restore relationships with those we blamed for our problems. This exercise will help you reflect on your increased responsibility or accountability for your problems. Fill in the blanks to see how far you've come in your growth journey.

- I used to blame ____ for my problem(s).

  ____

- I've taken responsibility for my problem(s) by ________________________.

  ____

- I am accountable for my actions because ______________________________.

  ____

- By taking responsibility, I have seen changes in my life that include ________.

  ____

- Taking responsibility has made me feel ________________________________.

  ____

- The most valuable outcome in my life from taking responsibility has been

  ____.

Many of us can point to something that keeps us going in life: a motivating factor. Where does your motivation come from? Maybe it's a person, or something else. Write down how you can focus on that source to keep your motivation level high. Part of being successful involves engaging in motivating practices consistently, rather than trying to reengage after you've lost the desire to stay on track.

CONTINUED ▶

Keeping track of growth begins with small steps, not leaps. It's common to feel that you're taking one step forward and two back, and that's part of the change process. Keeping a log of your daily progress as you're getting started will allow you to see what's working. List a few specific actions you've taken each day to move toward your goal. They can be small, such as reading ten pages of a book if your goal is to read more.

DAY	GOAL/ACTION
Sunday	
Monday	
Tuesday	

CONTINUED ▶

DAY	GOAL/ACTION
Wednesday	
Thursday	
Friday	
Saturday	

FROM STAGNATION TO GROWTH

As you measure your growth, you'll notice that the words you use to describe yourself are improving. Before making changes, some people may view themselves as unmotivated or helpless, for example. But after taking steps to make changes, they might say they've become more motivated, empowered, and directed in their lives.

Think about the adjectives you would have used to describe yourself in the past. In the left-hand column, circle those that apply to you, and list any of your own. In the right-hand column, circle and list words you feel describe you now.

PAST DESCRIPTORS OF YOURSELF	CURRENT DESCRIPTORS OF YOURSELF
Angry	Happy
Biased	Positive
Blaming	Content
Depressed	Focused
Fearful	Self-accepting
Self-criticizing	Self-aware
Stuck	Determined
Unmotivated	Satisfied

Reflect on these lists and think about how far you've come! Consider the additional steps you need to take to keep moving forward and list them. Then describe two or three ways you can implement these steps to maintain your momentum on your journey.

Getting another person's opinion about your progress often can help you see what you may have overlooked. Consider asking someone you trust to provide observations about the changes you're trying to make. Write down this person's name and when you can approach them. Ask them to offer an honest opinion of how they think you're doing and to give you any feedback they think would be useful to you.

CONTINUED ▶

MORE REWARDS PLEASE

You've been doing a lot of great work on yourself! Let's have a more detailed look at your reward system to help you stay motivated. Planning rewards as a regular part of your change routine can be great for maintaining motivation. Rewards can be little things you enjoy, like a favorite drink or snack. You can plan one reward at the end of the day or week and an even bigger reward at the end of the month. For example, if you're practicing an instrument or sports skill, you might set a daily reward of having a favorite drink after practice. If you practice daily for the entire week, you might treat yourself to your favorite lunch. You can plan an even bigger reward for practicing all month. Fill in your reward ideas in the section that follows.

- My daily reward for achieving my goal is ___________________________________.

- My weekly reward for achieving my goal is ___________________________________.

- My monthly reward for achieving my goal is ___________________________________.

Celebrating steps toward progress with rewards can help you stay motivated.
However, sometimes rewards you set early on no longer work. As you work on your
goals, think about the rewards you created initially. Do they still serve as motivators for
change? If not, make a list of new rewards.

Think about how far you've come. No matter how insignificant it might seem to you, write down advice you might give someone starting a similar change journey. Describe what worked and what didn't and highlight what you believe to be most important about this process. This will help you see how much progress you've made as well as the valuable lessons you've learned through this change process.

Our growth usually affects our self-esteem in positive ways. Consider your current successes. Think about positive feelings as they relate to the action steps you've taken and list them. Maybe you feel, proud, excited, encouraged, motivated, or something else. Write down specifically *when* you experience these feelings. Knowing what prompts good feelings will help you increase them. Say, for example, you feel proud when you exercise daily.

Consider enlisting another person to also embark on a journey to positive change. You can support each other and maybe even develop a healthy competition. If you and a friend are both trying to get healthier and more fit, for example, you can schedule workouts together and exchange healthy recipes to stay motivated and measure progress. List some people who could be potential "change buddies" and come up with a plan to approach them.

PART V

Tackling Obstacles and Failing Well

Fall down seven times, stand up eight.

—JAPANESE PROVERB

You're well on your way to change and growth, and you've gained a number of skills so far by doing the needed work on yourself. But do you sometimes feel like you're making little or no progress? It can seem like as soon as you're making progress, something pushes you back to old patterns. For example, you start a healthy eating routine but as soon as you pass a fast-food restaurant, you stop for a burger. Some factors might seem beyond your control no matter how much effort you put in; you might begin to lose motivation and begin to develop self-doubt as a result. This is not uncommon. Don't get discouraged! You *can* break the old patterns and stay on track, and this part shows you how. Falling down can be a teaching point for getting back up. You can recognize the triggers that knock you off your feet and develop a plan to counteract them. Remember, any important journey is often long and full of challenges, but reaching the destination will make it all worth it.

Looking closely at your change process can help you move forward. If it seems like change is going more slowly than you'd like, start by examining yourself. Determine whether you're being honest with yourself and consider whether you really want to change. List a few reasons that you might be resisting change. Examine this list and put a checkmark next to those that are within your control.

In the previous prompt, you examined reasons you might be resisting change. Look back and see how many are within your control. Reflect on where you tend to lose track of your goal and engage in behaviors that counteract your efforts (for example, buying cigarettes when you want to quit smoking). Write down an alternative plan (for example, consider wearing a nicotine patch). If one way isn't working, find another.

WHEN YOU ASSUME . . .

It can be easy to make unrealistic assumptions about our problems. For example, let's say you've convinced yourself that you'll never be on time for work because your life is just too hectic. Such assumptions can keep us from achieving our goals because they discourage us from trying to change. Our thinking process deeply influences the way we perceive our problems and how we formulate their solutions. This exercise helps you reflect on how you can counteract your assumptions by stating their opposites. Key to achieving goals is dispelling beliefs or false assumptions about what it means to make changes.

LIST AT LEAST THREE ASSUMPTIONS ABOUT YOUR PROBLEM	LIST THE OPPOSITE OF EACH ASSUMPTION TO COUNTERACT IT
1.	1.
2.	2.
3.	3.

To help you correct your faulty assumptions, consider enlisting the help of someone you trust. Write down this person's name. Ask them to reflect on your problem and help challenge any of your assumptions. After your conversation, jot down some thoughts about how they see your problem and what you've learned.

When you're getting started, leaning on people in your support system and telling them specifically what you need can be a big help. Say you're spending too much money. You can ask someone you trust to keep your cash and credit cards, describing exactly what you need. Write down the person's name and when you'll ask them for help.

Consider whether one of your obstacles on this change journey is your own tendency to deceive yourself or rationalize your behavior. Picture some of the times you reverted to old habits. Make a list of the excuses you made. Excuses can help us feel better, but they don't move us forward. Evaluate how what you tell yourself about why you're reverting keeps you from changing. Jot down how each keeps you stuck.

____

____

____

____

____

____

____

____

____

____

____

Are your impulses keeping you from meeting your goals? Many of us act on impulse to get that immediate reward. Let's say you've decided to declutter your basement, but just as you head down to get started you realize your favorite show is coming on in fifteen minutes, so you head back upstairs to watch instead. It's helpful to evaluate impulses and learn to delay gratification to give yourself time between the impulse and the behavior. If you really want to watch that show, make a deal with yourself that you'll spend the fifteen minutes working in the basement and then reassess your impulse. If you still want it at that point, then head upstairs.

In some cases, waiting for what your impulse is driving you to do can be difficult. Say your impulse is to go to a bakery when you've sworn off sweets. It may be helpful in such situations to give yourself a pause in some of the following ways. Check off those items in the list that appeal to you.

☐ Play a game on your phone or tablet

☐ Take a walk

☐ Watch TV

☐ Call a friend

☐ Read a book

☐ Take a shower

☐ Listen to music

☐ Go to sleep/take a nap

☐ Work on a project or hobby

☐ Fill in your own delaying gratification technique

____

____

____

Part of the change process is being able to forgive yourself when you fail. If you've tried to change a number of times without success, consider whether you're being too hard on yourself. The upside is that there are always lessons to be learned, and giving yourself grace is important. Describe what your perceived failure has taught you about yourself so far, focusing on your character and determination.

CONTINUED ▶

Consider your priorities. Some of us would say that we prioritize our families; others might put their career at the top of the list. Priorities keep us committed to our responsibilities. Make a list of your top three to five priorities and consider where your goal for change lies on this list. If changing is not among your top priorities, make a plan to move it up.

____

____

____

____

____

____

____

____

____

____

____

CONTINUED ▶

Sometimes we're afraid to succeed because success can bring certain losses. Write down a list of things you're afraid you'll lose when you change; perhaps friends come to mind or a sense of comfort. Next to each, note how you've been negatively impacted. What will continue happening if nothing changes? Make a plan to say goodbye so that you can move forward with your life.

____

____

____

____

____

____

____

____

____

____

____

____

____

CONTINUED ▶

When you think of your past mistakes, do you feel like some are unforgivable? Have you hurt someone so much that there's no going back? Do you believe the relationship is broken? Perhaps you're seeking forgiveness but are afraid to ask. If your goal is asking for forgiveness, write down what you have to lose if you go forward. Then, describe what you might lose if you don't.

____

____

____

____

____

____

____

____

____

____

____

CONTINUED ▶

You might feel like you've failed when you can't find a total solution to your problem or when your approach doesn't work right away, or at all. Let's say you're trying to stop eating junk food. After a week of healthy eating, you eat a bag of potato chips. Afterward, you might think that you should just give up. But remember that you didn't eat junk food for a whole week! The behavior you want to change didn't develop in a day, and it will take time to change it. This exercise will help you reflect on failure and look at your situation in a more positive and effective way.

How do you define failure?

____

____

____

Is your definition realistic? Explain why or why not.

____

____

____

Think about the ideas you've come up with so far to address the behavior you want to change. Have they moved you closer to where you want to be? What have you learned from any failed attempts?

____

____

____

There's one key ingredient to persistence and achieving the changes you want: patience. It gives you perspective, because when you try and fail, you learn a new way to try harder and better. Consider your level of patience with yourself. Write down the time frame you've given yourself to accomplish your goal and include a description of the progress you've made so far. Reflect on whether the amount of time you've given yourself is realistic. Return to this prompt periodically and adjust time frames based on your evaluations.

THROW IT AWAY

Carefully consider whether you're trying to address a problem by taking an approach that doesn't work (yet you stick with the approach over and over). For example, you're trying to stop eating donuts, but you continue buying them every time you go to the grocery store. Despite your intentions, you're continuing to engage in the same behavior. This exercise will help you think about how you can break behaviors that don't work and replace them with new ones.

Describe the solution you originally came up with to make a change in your life.

____

____

____

How many times have you tried this solution? Why do you think it doesn't seem to be working?

____

____

____

What different solution or replacement behavior can you think of? Get creative. If you have more than one, test each to see which is more effective.

____

____

____

When you're going through hell, keep going.

—ANONYMOUS

Change might require you to do things you don't like. Maybe you really dislike exercising, but you know it's good for you. Try the "fake it 'til you make it" approach and use positive self-talk. Tell yourself, "I can do this" and push yourself to turn any dread into "This won't be so bad." Write down your "fake it 'til you make it" statements and when to use them.

CONTINUED ▶

When change is hard, it can be helpful to look at the big picture of your life and evaluate how you want people to remember you once you're gone. Our morals, values, actions, and interactions with people we come into contact with leave our mark in the world. How does the way you are in life now differ from what you'd like people to remember about you? This exercise will help you put things into perspective.

Looking at your life right now, what do you think people will remember about you when you're gone?

____

____

Do you think your life could be used as an example to anyone? If so, what kind of example?

____

____

How do you want people to remember you?

____

____

If you want people's memories of you when you're no longer here to be different than what they would be right now, what changes are needed?

____

____

PART VI

Practicing Self-Love

*One cannot get through life without pain. What we can do
is choose how to use the pain life presents to us.*

—BERNIE S. SIEGEL

You have braved this journey to a better you. Through this process, you've
learned more about yourself. You've had successes and failures as so many
people do. An important ingredient in a successful change process is loving
yourself enough to give yourself permission to learn and grow from your failures. Allow yourself to celebrate and take joy in your successes! Loving yourself
means that you're kind to yourself and care for *you*, which can mean that your
needs come first. Self-love is knowing your own self-worth and looking out for
when you need to take care of yourself in order to be able to care for others later.
This last part of the journal helps guide reflections on self-love, self-care, forgiving yourself, and encouraging yourself to move forward. This section is one of
the most important of the journal, and one that I hope will stay with you long
after you've put it down.

Reflect on self-love. Is this a concept you grew up with? Think about whether self-love was discussed when you were a child. Was it encouraged by adults in your life? Perhaps you were told to take care of yourself, rest, eat healthy, take breaks, and ask for help when needed. Write down the lessons you learned about self-love from your parents, caregivers, teachers, or other adults.

SELF-CARE CHECKLIST

In reflecting on self-care, think about what you do for yourself. Can you list at least three ways you care for yourself, including giving yourself time for relaxation? (If you find it difficult to come up with some ideas, it might be time to practice more self-care!) Use the following list to check off what you already do or as ideas for what you can do. Circle those items you'd like to start doing. What seems appealing or relaxing to you?

☐ Read a book ☐ Meditate

☐ Listen to music ☐ Work on a hobby

☐ Exercise ☐ Plan a vacation or trip

☐ Take a bath ☐ Take a nap

☐ Take a walk ☐ Talk to a friend

☐ Get a massage ☐ Go for a car ride

☐ Watch a movie ☐ Write down what you're grateful for

☐ Eat your favorite food ☐ Play with your pet

☐ Paint your nails or shave ☐ Look through pictures

☐ Go out with friends ☐ Declutter or tidy a space

____

____

*Self-compassion is simply giving the same kindness
to ourselves that we would give to others.*

—CHRISTOPHER GERMER

Part of self-love and taking care of yourself is believing you deserve it. Reflect on whether you believe you deserve to care for yourself and think about how your self-love affects the changes you want to make in your life. Do you feel you deserve to treat yourself better? Write down your thoughts about being worthy of making changes to improve your life. Consider whether your perceptions might be holding you back.

____

____

____

____

____

____

____

____

____

CONTINUED ▶

It's helpful to remember that people still love you and care about your well-being and happiness regardless of how many mistakes you've made. You might question whether this is the case, but it's true. It can be helpful to think periodically about what people in your life do to show you love. Gestures of love don't have to be big; they matter because they make you feel good. No matter how small the act of kindness, it's important to remember that it was directed toward you because you matter. This exercise will help you remember those acts of kindness that show love of you.

List three to five people you care about whose love you want.

1. ____

2. ____

3. ____

4. ____

5. ____

What have these individuals done to show you they care about you? Remember the little things, like a hug or phone call to check up on you. These are all acts that show they care.

- Person 1: _______________________________________

- Person 2: _______________________________________

- Person 3: _______________________________________

- Person 4: _______________________________________

- Person 5: _______________________________________

Forgiveness is an important part of moving forward in your life. Reflect on your ability to forgive. Was forgiveness encouraged when you were growing up? Do you forgive others, or do you tend to hang on to what you perceive as their wrongdoings? Consider how this pattern carries over to forgiving yourself. Describe your ability to forgive yourself for your mistakes, and reflect on how this might contribute to progress or setbacks in your life.

FORGIVENESS LETTER TO SELF

Think about some of your behaviors that you don't feel very good about. For example, you made a promise to your friend and broke it, which then strained your relationship. You feel terrible about this, and the guilt is eating away at you. It's time to write a letter of forgiveness to yourself. People make mistakes, and holding on to guilt will only hold you back from living your life to the fullest. Find some time to sit in a quiet place and reflect. Start the letter with something like, "Dear Self." Describe what you can't forgive yourself for and include how you felt during that time. Consider how not forgiving yourself has held you back. Then write down why it's time to forgive yourself for your behavior. Remember, you deserve to be happy, too. It's okay to own your mistakes and move on.

Often, we're our own worst critic. Think about your inner voice. Does it tend to be complimentary and encouraging or disparaging? If the latter, try identifying the point where the voice starts to become critical. Is it when you make a mistake? Or maybe the criticism starts before any wrongdoing on your part to sabotage your success. Writing down these exact points will help you recognize and break your patterns.

CONTINUED ▶

Think about the most important role you play in someone's life. Are you a spouse, part-ner, parent, caregiver, or friend? Consider what you already do in this role that makes you feel good about yourself. For example, as a parent, you may feel that you're patient with your children. Make a list of what you do in this role and reflect on those qualities that are positive.

CONTINUED ▶

Within every role you play (child, parent, partner, sibling, friend, etc.) is goodness. Your positive acts have had an impact, no matter how small, on someone's life. Think of ways you have affected someone you care about: maybe driving your child to their soccer game or bringing a meal to a grandparent. This exercise will help you reflect on the positive impact you've made on the lives of other people. Fill in those that apply.

- As a child, I made a positive impact on my parents by _______________________.

- As a grandchild, I made a positive impact on my grandparents by _______________.

- As a parent/caregiver, I made a positive impact on my child/children by ___________.

- As a partner/spouse, I made a positive impact by _______________________.

- As a friend, I made a positive impact by _______________________.

- As a co-worker, I made a positive impact by _______________________.

- As a _______________________ I made a positive

  impact by _______________________.

Now think about the role you play on a broader scale. Use the space that follows to reflect on the good you do for your community, your faith tradition or spiritual practice, the animals or plants that you care for, or even the health of the planet.

____

____

____

____

Everyone needs a break sometimes. Do you think you take enough breaks for self-care? If not, think about the schedule you keep. Perhaps you rush from one thing to the next or often get pulled away from doing something for yourself. List a few ways that you can fit self-care into your life on a daily, weekly, or monthly basis.

Think about the last time you expressed to someone else a need related to self-care. Maybe you asked your family to give you an hour to attend a group session or activity or to read a book. Consider the support you might need to make time for self-care activities in your busy schedule. Describe a specific plan with your family that allows time for self-care.

Part of caring for yourself is feeling a sense of security in your life; this can include security with yourself, your family, and your friends. Do you feel secure in your relationships? If you're afraid of losing someone you care about, what evidence do you have that this might actually happen? Describe what you need to feel secure and how you can get there.

____

____

____

____

____

____

____

____

____

____

____

____

Are you ready to let go of negative emotions? As you assess your inner feelings, think about negative emotions that come up more than you think they should. Maybe you're experiencing anger, anxiety, or sadness. Think about what could help you manage these emotions, such as engaging in distraction techniques, making amends with someone, or doing relaxation exercises. Write when and how you can implement these strategies to let those negative emotions go.

You've probably heard the saying, "What doesn't kill you makes you stronger." Reflect on your journey so far. How have the problems you've confronted helped you build skills, character, or feelings of self-worth? Think about the lessons you've learned. Have you learned anything surprising about yourself? Think of one positive word or phrase you'd apply to yourself as it relates to your change process, reflecting on where you started and where you are today.

Self-care includes taking care of all your senses. This includes finding relaxation through all five senses if you have access to them: hearing, sight, smell, taste, and touch. This type of sensory kit can be your go-to when you need to unwind and relax. It's helpful to prepare so that it's ready when you need it. For example, you can keep a stress ball or soft blanket to appeal to your sense of touch. Stock your kitchen with your favorite tea or cold drink to appeal to your sense of taste. Come up with your list of sensory items and jot them down in the space that follows.

1. A sensory item that appeals to my sense of hearing is _________________________.

2. A sensory item that appeals to my sense of sight is _________________________.

3. A sensory item that appeals to my sense of smell is _________________________.

4. A sensory item that appeals to my sense of taste is _________________________.

5. A sensory item that appeals to my sense of touch is _________________________.

RESOURCES

Anxiety & Depression Association of America

adaa.org

Provides information on understanding anxiety and depression and related disorders as well as resources on obtaining help.

Calm App

calm.com

App for sleep and meditation. Provides sleep stories, guided meditations, and a music library.

Children and Adults with Attention Deficit/Hyperactivity Disorder (CHADD)

chadd.org

Provides education and resources for individuals and families whose lives have been touched by ADHD.

***The Gigantic Book of Famous Quotations*, by Joanne Kelly**

Provides inspirational quotes. Good for keeping motivated and staying positive.

National Eating Disorders Association

nationaleatingdisorders.org

Dedicated to supporting individuals and family members who have been affected by eating disorders.

National Institute of Mental Health

nimh.nih.gov

Provides information and resources on mental illness for diagnosed individuals and for families and caregivers.

National Suicide Prevention Lifeline

1-800-273-TALK (8255), suicidepreventionlifeline.org

Operates twenty-four hours a day, 365 days a year. Provides free and confidential support for people in distress and crisis.

Substance Abuse and Mental Health Services Administration

samhsa.gov

Provides information and resources on mental health and substance use treatment, including treatment locators by city and zip code.

REFERENCES

"Big Five Inventory, BFI-2-S (Short)." Big Five Inventory, BFI-2-S (short). Online version. Accessed May 16, 2022. https://psytests.org/bigfive/bfi2sen.html.

Coles, Nicholas A., Jeff T. Larsen, and Heather C. Lench. "A Meta-Analysis of the Facial Feedback Literature: Effects of Facial Feedback on Emotional Experience Are Small and Variable." *Psychological Bulletin* 145, no. 6 (2019): 610–651. doi: 10.1037/bul0000194.

Cooper, John O., Timothy E. Heron, and William L. Heward. *Applied Behavior Analysis.* 3rd ed. New Jersey: Pearson, 2020.

de Shazer, Steve, and Yvonne Dolan, with Harry Korman, Terry Trepper, Eric McCollum, and Insoo Kim Berg. *More Than Miracles: The State of the Art of Solution-Focused Brief Therapy.* New York: Routledge, 2021.

Doran, G. T. (1981). There's a S.M.A.R.T. Way to Write Management's Goals and Objectives. Management Review, 70, 35–36.

"Hogan Personality Inventory." Hogan Assessments, October 21, 2021. https://www.hoganassessments.com/assessment/hogan-personality-inventory/.

Lamoreux, Karen. "What Is the Minnesota Multiphasic Personality Inventory (MMPI)?" Psych Central. Psych Central, April 29, 2022. https://psychcentral.com/lib /minnesota-multiphasic-personality-inventory-mmpi.

McCrae, Robert R, and Paul T. Costa. *Personality in Adulthood: A Five-Factor Theory Perspective*. New York: Guilford Press, 2003.

The Myers & Briggs Foundation - MBTI® basics. Accessed May 16, 2022. https://www .myersbriggs.org/my-mbti-personality-type/mbti-basics/.

INDEX

A

accountability, 27, 92

action plan

  implementing, 55, 62, 75

  setting, 66

  strategies, 42, 68

affirmations, 58

alcohol

  effects of, 10

  stop drinking, 73

anxiety, reducing, 30, 58, 160

assumptions, false, 116–117

attention, gaining, 31

avoidance, 1, 31–32, 61, 86

B

behavior

  action steps, 75

  behavior change contract, 76

  changing patterns of, 10, 13, 30, 42, 75, 86, 131

  consequences of, 61, 114, 148

  impulsive, 122

  main functions of, 31

  patterns of, 55, 120, 134

  positive changes, 32

blame, casting to others, 17, 92

C

change

  awareness of, 4, 10, 25

  changes that work/last, 35

  emotional, 10, 77

  future self, picturing, 33, 137

  implementing, 23, 47, 71, 75

  planning for, 30, 70

  relationship, 25, 30, 51, 64, 86

  resisting, 112, 114, 134–135

contract, behavior
     change, 76
Cooper, John, 31

D

discouragement, 83, 111

E

emotions
   controlling/managing, 19, 37
   fake it til you make
      it, 77, 135
   negative, 92, 160

F

failure
   feelings of, 131
   learning from, 139
   perceived, 123
fear
   of change, 30
   of loss, 66
   of success, 70, 127
   of what others
      think, 62
forgiveness
   letter to self, 148
   of past mistakes, 129, 146

G

goals
   achievement of, 51–52, 62
   motivation, 43, 56
      See also motivation
   S.M.A.R.T., 39–40
   setting, 27, 37, 43, 49
goodness, 153
growth
   measuring, 86, 97
   responsibility
      for, 70, 92
   results of, 106, 111
   tracking, 83, 95–96

H

habits
   changing, 61, 87
   forming new, 55
   old, 23, 42, 73, 120
happiness scale, 59
Heron, Timothy E., 31
Heward, William, 31

I

impulsive behavior, 122

K

kindness, acts of, 145, 153

M

mindset, 43, 58

mistakes, 129, 145–146, 148

motivation

  and goals, 43, 56

  maintaining, 83–84, 101, 111

  source of, 93, 108

moving forward, 20, 90, 98, 146

N

negativity, letting go of, 58, 92, 127, 160

O

obstacles, overcoming, 42, 111, 120

opinion, of others, as

    positive, 99

P

patience, 132

performance, increasing, 58

personality

  characteristics, 2

  concerns of, 4

  qualities, 2, 5, 151

  traits, 70

priorities, 125

problems

  accountability for, 92, 162

  assumptions of, 116

progress

  accountability for, 37, 40, 95, 99, 108

  celebrating, 102, 104

  measuring, 27, 39, 45, 75–76, 83

  reflecting on, 86, 132, 146

  sabotaging/hindering, 35, 42, 70, 90, 111

purpose, 13, 27

R

reflections

  positive changes, 162

  on progress, 84, 86, 98

  self-care, 139–140, 143, 156

  self-reflection, 9, 92, 114, 116, 131, 139

relationships

  changing, 25, 30, 51, 66, 86

  feeling of security, 158

  healing, 15, 64, 92

relaxation, 142, 160, 164

resources, 166–167

responsibility, 92

rewards, system of, 101–102

S

self-awareness, 4

self-care, 154, 156, 158, 164

self-esteem, 51, 58, 79, 84, 89, 106

self-love

  is forgiveness, 148–149

practicing, 139, 143, 153
  reflecting on, 140, 151, 162
self-portrait, past/present, 89
self-talk, your inner voice, 58, 90, 135, 149
self-worth, 139, 151, 162
sensory kit, 164
setbacks, 42, 87, 146
shortcuts, 95
solutions, 116
strengths, awareness of, 70, 86

success
  fear of, 127
  increasing likelihood of, 39, 49, 139
  plan for, 55, 123
  what it looks like, 25, 35
support system, 4, 20, 42, 66, 108, 118

W

who are you
  reflecting on your past, 1–2

ACKNOWLEDGMENTS

Thank you to my husband, Paul and my son, Christian.
Their love and support made writing this book possible.

ABOUT THE AUTHOR

Agnes Ward, PhD, is a licensed psychologist, certified advanced alcohol and drug counselor, and licensed behavior analyst. She has provided psychotherapy to children, adults, and families. Her focus is on treating trauma, postpartum depression, self-injury, and eating disorders. She has presented to clinical professionals, educators, and spiritual groups on the effects of trauma across the life span, eating disorders, human trafficking, and self-injury. Dr. Ward enjoys spending time with her family, reading, and taking family vacations.